THE TOP OF THE WORLD

OF THE

WORLD

Climbing Mount Everest

BY STEVE JENKINS

HOUGHTON MIFFLIN COMPANY   BOSTON

For Jamie, Alec, and Page

Library of Congress Cataloging-in-Publication Data

Jenkins, Steve, 1952–
The top of the world : climbing Mount Everest / Steve Jenkins.
p.   cm.
Summary: Describes the conditions and terrain of Mount Everest, attempts that have been made
to scale this peak, and general information about the equipment and techniques of mountain climbing.
RNF ISBN 0-395-94218-7 PAP ISBN 0-618-19676-5
1. Mountaineering—Everest, Mount (China and Nepal)—Juvenile literature. [1. Everest, Mount
(China and Nepal) 2. Mountaineering.] I. Title. II. Title: Climbing Mount Everest.
GV199.44.E85J45   1999
796.52'2'095496-dc21   98-42748 CIP AC

Printed in Malaysia
TWP 20 19 18 17 16 15 14

Mount Everest

Its summit is the highest point on earth, 5½ miles above sea level. For thousands of years, the mountain has been a sacred place for those who live in its shadow. The rest of the world, however, wasn't really aware of the mountain until about 180 years ago. Ever since that time, climbers, scientists, and adventurers have been fascinated by this peak. Many have tried to climb it. Some have succeeded, but many more have failed. Some have died trying.

Mount Everest is a place of great beauty, adventure, and danger. If you ever want to climb it, here are a few things to think about.

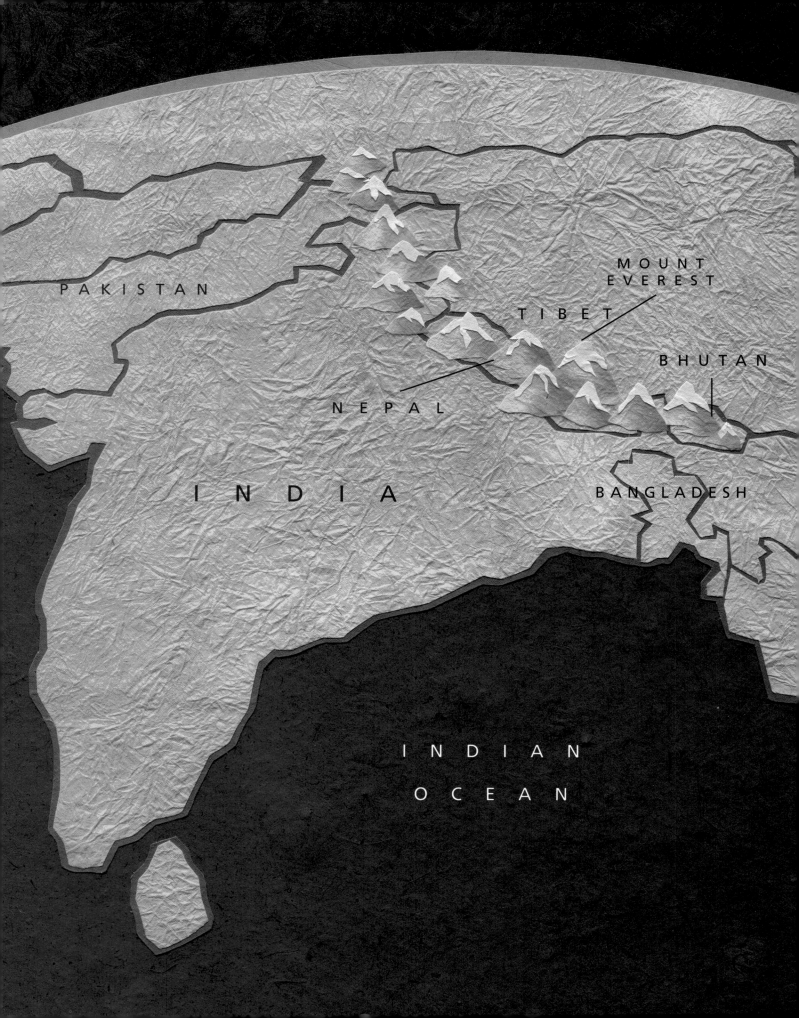

The Roof of the World

Rising between India and China, the Himalayas are the highest mountain range on earth. More than 1,500 miles long, the range includes many of the world's tallest peaks. The highest of them all, Mount Everest, stands on the border of Nepal and Tibet. Its summit is 29,028 feet above sea level.

Nepal, a small country that borders India, is the home of the Sherpa people. Tibet is an ancient country that is now part of China. People in Nepal and Tibet think of Mount Everest as a holy place, full of power and mystery.

CHINA

Continental Drift

The earth's continents are always moving, drifting slowly together or apart. One hundred million years ago, an ocean separated what is now India from the rest of Asia. About forty million years ago, India plowed into the Asian continent. This collision is still going on. India is moving north at about 2½ inches a year, pushing up the Himalayan Mountains as it goes.

The earth, one hundred million years ago

THE HIMALAYAS

INDIAN SUBCONTINENT

ASIA

Measuring the Mountain

In the 1820s, British surveyors set out to map and measure the Himalayas. They were not allowed to enter Nepal or Tibet, so they were forced to take measurements from as much as one hundred miles away. Still, they were able to determine the height of Everest, then known to the British as Peak 15, with remarkable accuracy.

Namesake

Peak 15 was renamed in honor of Sir George Everest, the first leader of the British survey, a mapping expedition to the Himalayas. The Nepalese call the mountain Sagarmatha. The Tibetan name, Chomolungma, means "Mother Goddess of the World."

Flying In

Most expeditions to the Himalayas begin with a plane flight to Kathmandu, the capital of Nepal. Passenger jets cruise at about the same altitude as Everest's summit.

Kathmandu

When you arrive in the bustling capital city of Nepal, you'll collect your gear, meet your guides, and pay for your climbing permit. If you're lucky, you'll have time to pay a visit to the Monkey Temple, one of the many Buddhist religious sites in the city. Sherpas and other climbers often make offerings here before beginning an expedition.

Kathmandu is also where you'll begin the long trek to Everest.

The Sherpas

Since the first British adventurers came to Nepal, a group of native people known as Sherpas have worked with climbers as guides and partners. They are famous for their strength, climbing skill, and honesty. Sherpas are born and raised in the mountains, so they are accustomed to the altitude and can work well high on the mountain.

Land of the Yak

Many Sherpas live by raising yaks, animals that are closely related to cattle. Yaks can withstand the harsh cold of the mountains and are often used to help carry expedition supplies to base camp.

First to the Top

The British expedition of 1921 was the first organized attempt to climb Mount Everest. Sickness and exhaustion kept the climbers from reaching the top, but they did discover a route to the summit. Many attempts by climbers of different nationalities followed, but no one succeeded until May 29, 1953, when Edmund Hillary and Tenzing Norgay reached the summit. Hillary was from New Zealand and Tenzing Norgay was a Sherpa from Nepal. Both men became international heroes.

Because It's There

In 1924, British climbers George Mallory and Andrew Irvine attempted to climb Everest, and were last seen climbing just below the summit. No one knows if they reached the top before they disappeared. When asked why he wanted to climb the mountain, Mallory gave his famous reply: "Because it's there."

Mallory and Irvine were last seen here.

The Greatest Climber

In 1980, the Austrian climber Reinhold Messner accomplished what was considered an impossible feat. He climbed Mount Everest alone, without bottled oxygen. Messner was also the first to climb all of the fourteen peaks in the world that are higher than 8,000 meters (26,247 feet). He is considered by many to be the greatest mountaineer of all time.

Packing for the Trip

It takes a lot of special gear to climb Mount Everest. Here is some of the equipment you'll need.

Climbing Suit

Worn as the outermost of several layers, this down-filled one-piece suit can keep you warm at temperatures of $-100°F$.

Glacier Glasses

The sun is dangerously bright at high altitudes, especially when reflected by snow. Even a few minutes without eye protection can result in painful eye burns and make you temporarily snow-blind.

Mittens

The inner and outer layers keep your hands warm and dry. The mittens must be extremely warm but flexible enough for you to use an ice ax and other tools.

Crampons

These sets of sharp metal spikes attach to your boots to give you secure footing on icy surfaces.

Trekking Poles

Used for balance, the poles can be adjusted in length for different kinds of terrain.

Mountaineering Boots

These boots have a plastic outer shell and several layers of insulation to keep your feet warm and dry.

Jumar

A device used in climbing a rope; a jumar slips easily up but cannot slide down.

Ropes

On Everest, the guides or lead climbers anchor the rope above steep and dangerous sections of the route. Climbers attach themselves to the rope for safety.

Backpack

You'll need a good backpack to carry food, climbing equipment, and extra clothes. Since it's dangerous to remove your mittens for even a moment in extreme cold, the zippers and storage compartments must be easy to operate.

Sleeping Bag

Down-filled and warm enough for the bitter cold of the mountain, a good sleeping bag is essential for surviving the nights on Everest.

Radio

The members of a climbing party use radios to stay in contact with each other and to call for help in an emergency.

Stove

A reliable stove melts snow into drinking water and allows climbers to make hot tea.

Ice Ax

This multipurpose tool can be held like a walking stick for balance, used like a pick to cut footholds in the ice, or driven into the snow to keep you from sliding down the mountain after a fall. Stopping a slide in this way is called a "self-arrest."

Shovel

The shovel acts as an anchor in deep snow, and is used to clear tents after snowstorms and to dig out climbers buried by avalanches.

Oxygen Mask and Tank

All but the strongest and most experienced climbers must use extra oxygen at the mountain's higher altitudes.

Tent

It's important to take a strongly built tent with a streamlined shape that can withstand the gale-force winds and shed the heavy snow you'll probably experience on the mountain.

Home Away from Home

Mount Everest's severe cold, high winds, and heavy snowfall make the climb possible only during a few weeks in the spring and late summer. During those times, as many as several hundred climbers, guides, doctors, Sherpas, cooks, and others live in base camp, a tent city at the foot of the mountain. Waiting here for your chance to climb the mountain helps your body to acclimate, or get used to the lack of oxygen in the air.

Blessings of the Gods

The Sherpas are Buddhists and are very religious. They consider the mountain sacred and won't start up without a *Puja*, a ceremony to ask the gods for protection and permission to climb.

The World's Highest Dump

Several attempts have been made to clean up the mountain over the past few years. Still, at base camp and other, higher camps on Everest, one finds thousands of empty oxygen bottles, discarded climbing gear, tents destroyed by the weather, and even the bodies of some of the climbers who have died on the mountain.

The Icefall

The most popular climbing route from base camp to the top of Everest, the South Summit route, passes through the Khumbu icefall. The icefall is created by the Khumbu glacier as it flows over a steep section of the mountain. Because the glacier moves two or three feet each day, the icefall is one of the most dangerous and frightening parts of the climb. Deep cracks, or crevasses, are constantly opening and closing. Huge towers of ice, called séracs, can topple over without warning. You have to cross many sections of the icefall on shaky aluminum ladders placed by the Sherpas.

Rivers of Ice

As snow accumulates on a mountain slope over a period of years, it turns to ice and begins moving down the mountain. This moving mass of snow and ice is called a glacier. Much of the landscape of the Himalayas has been formed by glaciers as they carve out valleys and grind away rocks.

Gasping for Breath

Less oxygen in each breath means you have to breathe much faster. Everyone at very high altitudes feels tired, dizzy, and weak. Some people may have more serious problems: their lungs or brain stop working properly. If this happens, they must descend to a lower altitude immediately, or they may die.

Summit
29,028 feet

MOUNT
EVEREST

THE
SOUTH COL
ROUTE

Up and Down

At 29,000 feet, there is only one third as much oxygen as at sea level. In fact, if someone at sea level were suddenly transported to the top of Everest, he or she would die within a few minutes from the lack of oxygen. To prepare for the extremely thin air, you must make several round trips from base camp to higher and higher points on the mountain, sometimes spending the night before starting back down. Staying for increasing periods of time high on the mountain helps keep you from getting altitude sickness on summit day.

Camp 4
26,000 feet

Camp 3
24,000 feet

Camp 2
21,300 feet

Camp 1
19,500 feet

I C E
F A L L

K H U M B U
G L A C I E R

Base Camp
17,600 feet

T O
K A T H M A N D U

Unstable Layers

Avalanches occur when one layer of snow slides easily over another or when water under the snow makes the mountain's surface slippery.

crack formed by a slab of snow beginning to break loose

new snow

old snow with an icy surface

Avalanche!

When snowfall builds up on a steep mountainside, a whole section of a slope may break loose suddenly and slide down the mountain, moving at speeds of up to 200 miles per hour. More climbers on Mount Everest are killed by avalanches than by anything else.

Hold On

Mount Everest is so tall that it's affected by the jet stream, a narrow, fast-moving air current that circles the world six to ten miles above sea level.

High winds on the mountain make climbing — and surviving — much more difficult. Blowing snow can make it difficult to see, and wind-chill makes the low temperatures feel even colder. The winds are so strong at times that climbers have actually been blown right off the mountain.

Snow Plume

The jet stream, moving at speeds up to 250 mph, often causes clouds to form over the summit of Mount Everest. Its winds can blow plumes of snow several thousand feet long off the mountain.

Brrr!

The constant cold adds to the challenge of high-altitude mountain climbing. At the top of Everest, typical high temperatures in summer are around −20°F. Nighttime temperatures of −100°F are common. To make matters worse, when there's less oxygen available, it's much harder to stay warm. Well-insulated clothes are a matter of life or death on the mountain.

Frostbite

Sometimes climbers' hands, feet, or faces get so cold that they freeze. This condition, called frostbite, often results in the loss of the parts of the body that have frozen. Many high-altitude climbers have lost fingers or toes in this way.

The Death Zone

Above 26,000 feet, there is so little oxygen that climbers' bodies can't adapt. Anyone who remains at this elevation will get weaker and weaker and eventually die. That's why, once they reach this altitude, climbers have to get to the summit within a day or two. If they don't, they must descend to a lower camp.

Summit Day

It can take more than twelve hours to climb to the top from Camp 4. Since it's critical to make it back to camp before dark, climbers usually set out before midnight, and climb through the night by the light of a headlamp. With luck, these climbers will be on top the following noon.

The Summit

When you stand on top of Mount Everest, you are the highest thing on earth. For most people, reaching this point is the reward for years of hard work and planning. You can't stay long, though. Your body needs oxygen, which means getting back to a lower altitude quickly. Because you're so exhausted, the descent is one of the most dangerous parts of the climb, so you'll have to be very careful on the way down.

The Seven Summits

The tallest mountain on each of the seven continents, in feet

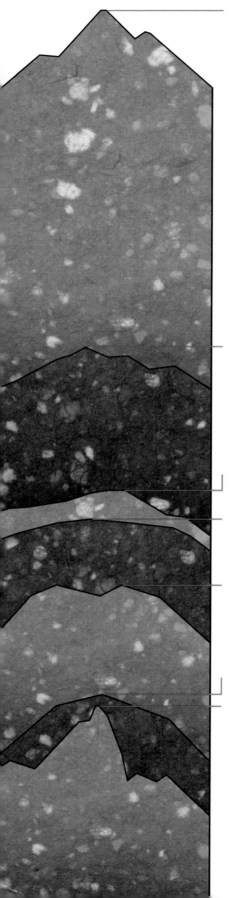

Asia: Everest 29,028

South America:
Aconcagua 22,835

North America:
Denali   20,320

Africa: Kilimanjaro 19,340

Europe: Elbrus 18,350

Antarctica: Vinson 16,066

Australia/Oceania:
Djaja 16,022

Mount Everest Records

First ascent: Edmund Hillary and Tenzing Norgay, May 29, 1953

First ascent by a woman: Junko Tabei, May 16, 1975

First ascent without bottled oxygen: Reinhold Messner and Peter Habeler, May 8, 1978

First solo ascent: Reinhold Messner, August 20, 1980

Most ascents: 10, by Ang Rita Sherpa

Largest number to reach the summit in a single day: 40, on May 10, 1993

Oldest climber to reach the top: 60

Youngest climber to reach the top: 16

Total number of ascents: 1,057

Number of climbers to die on the mountain: 161

Records are current as of January, 1999.
For up-to-date information visit:

Everest News at www.everestnews.com

Other informative Web sites:

www.mteverest.com

www.mountainzone.com/everest

Bibliography

Chris Bonington. *Mountaineer*.
San Francisco: Sierra Club Books, 1990.

Chris Bonington, Audrey Salkeld (eds).
Heroic Climbs.
Seattle: The Mountaineers, 1994.

Broughton Coburn.
Everest: Mountain Without Mercy.
National Geographic Society, 1997.

Roger Frisson-Roche and Sylvia Jouty.
A History of Mountain Climbing.
New York: Flammarion, 1996.

Roberto Mantovani.
Everest: History of the Himalayan Giant.
Seattle: The Mountaineers, 1997.

Reinhold Messner. *Free Spirit*.
Seattle: The Mountaineers, 1991.

Neil Morris. *Mountains*.
New York: Crabtree, 1996.

Galen Rowell. *The Art of Adventure*.
San Francisco: Sierra Club Books, 1996.

The Top of the World: Climbing Mount Everest

Boston Globe–Horn Book Award
ALA Notable Children's Books
NCTE-Orbis Pictus Recommended Nonfiction for Children Honor Book
School Library Journal "Best Books"
ALA Quick Picks for Reluctant Young Readers

Steve Jenkins lives in Boulder, Colorado, with his wife and three children. He has created many acclaimed books for Houghton Mifflin Company.

Also by Steve Jenkins:

Biggest, Strongest, Fastest
Looking Down
Big and Little
What Do You Do When Something Wants to Eat You?
Hottest, Coldest, Highest, Deepest
Slap, Squeak & Scatter: How Animals Communicate
Animals in Flight

Illustrated by Steve Jenkins:

Animal Dads written by Sneed Collard
Elephants Swim written by Linda Capus Riley
Making Animal Babies written by Sneed Collard

★ "Mount Everest may be imposing, but Steve Jenkins takes its measure in a strikingly executed picture book. . . . From start to finish, Jenkins has created a breathtaking tour-de-force."
—*Horn Book*, starred review

"An invigorating and fact-filled look at the great peak."
—*The Bulletin*

★ "Readers will cheer with the climber illustrated on the summit, and want to go back and pore over the details in the words and pictures again . . . [an] excellent example of pictorial nonfiction."
—*School Library Journal*, starred review

$6.95

SANDPIPER
HOUGHTON MIFFLIN
BOOKS

ISBN-13: 978-0-618-19676-0
ISBN-10: 0-618-19676-5

90000

9 780618 196760

Under the Ice

Kids Can Press acknowledges the financial support of the Ontario Arts Council, the Canada Council for the Arts and the Government of Canada, through the BPIDP, for our publishing activity.

Published in Canada by
Kids Can Press Ltd.
29 Birch Avenue
Toronto, ON M4V 1E2

Published in the U.S. by
Kids Can Press Ltd.
2250 Military Road
Tonawanda, NY 14150

www.kidscanpress.com

Written by Kathy Conlan, Louise Dickson, Iain Hunter
Edited by Valerie Wyatt and Charis Wahl
Designed by Julia Naimska
Printed and bound in China

The hardcover edition of this book is smyth sewn casebound.
The paperback edition of this book is limp sewn with a drawn-on cover.

CM 02 0 9 8 7 6 5 4 3 2
CM PA 04 0 9 8 7 6 5 4 3

National Library of Canada Cataloguing in Publication Data

Conlan, Kathleen Elizabeth, 1950–
        Under the ice

On cover: A Canadian Museum of Nature book.
ISBN 978-1-55337-001-7 (bound)
ISBN 978-1-55337-060-4 (pbk.)

1. Marine pollution — Polar Regions — Juvenile literature.
2. Marine biology — Polar regions — Juvenile literature.
3. Conlan, Kathy — Juvenile literature. 4. Marine biologists — Biography — Juvenile literature.
I. Dickson, Louise, 1959– II. Hunter, Iain
III. Title.

QH91.16.C65 2002   578.77'09163'2   C2001-904240-X

Kids Can Press is a *Corus*™ Entertainment company